Roundabouts

Our globe, our world

Kate Petty
and Jakki Wood

Sahara

WITHDRAWN

grassl

A & C Black • London

First published 1993
A & C Black (Publishers) Limited
35 Bedford Row
London WC1R 4JH

ISBN 0-7136-3709-9

© Aladdin Books Limited 1993
An Aladdin Book
designed and produced by
Aladdin Books Limited
28 Percy Street
London
WIP 9FF

A CIP catalogue record for this book
is available from the British Library

Printed in Belgium

Design David West
Children's Book Design
Illustration Jakki Wood
Text Kate Petty
Consultants Keith Lye B.A., F.R.S.G.,
Eva Bass Cert. Ed., teacher of
geography to 5-8 year-olds

Contents

Preparing for a journey

Greetings from Yorville.

Harry and his dog Ralph want to go to the seaside at Yorville. They look at a map to find out which is the easiest way to get there.

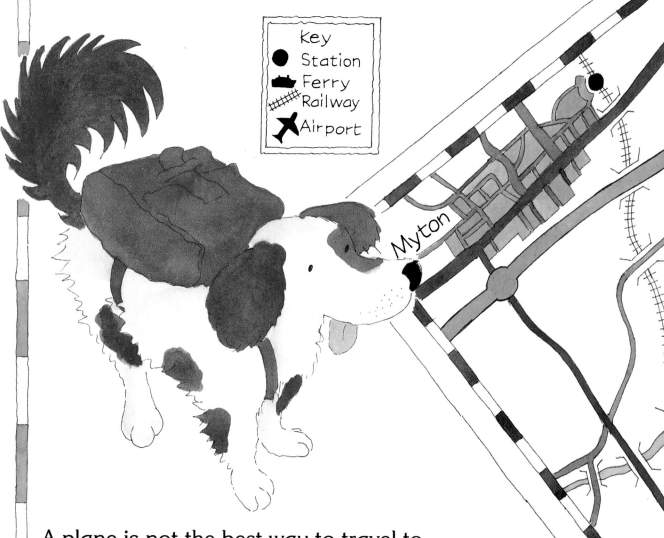

Key
- ● Station
- ⛴ Ferry
- ▦ Railway
- ✈ Airport

Myton

A plane is not the best way to travel to somewhere so near, and there isn't an airport close to Harry and Ralph's town anyway. If they go by train, they will have to take three different trains. If they go by road, how can they plan their journey or route?

By train, we'd have to change at Woodham, Camford and Creek to get from Myton to Yorville.

Yorville

Creek

Camford

Woodham

Find the quickest route to the seaside from where you live.

Road maps

Harry and Ralph look closely at the road map. Motorways are big roads with fast traffic. On the map, they are coloured blue. The main roads are coloured dark red or light red. The traffic on these roads is fast. Narrow roads are coloured brown.

Myton

Harry has planned most of the route from Myton to the seaside at Yorville.

Yorville

Creek

Camford

Woodham

Can you help Ralph plan the last part of the journey?

9

Where the land meets the sea

Here are Harry and Ralph at the seaside. They are on the edge of the land where it meets the sea. This is called the seashore or the coast.

Let's go and look at the horizon.

We'll never reach it but let's go anyway.

They walk along the coastal path. When they look into the distance, they seem to see the place where the sky meets the sea. This is called the horizon. They can't see any further because the Earth curves away from them.

Why can't Harry and Ralph visit the horizon?

Crossing the sea

Harry and Ralph fly over the sea in their balloon to reach the next bit of land. Can you think of any other ways of crossing the sea? As they fly, there's no land in sight, only sea. Most of the world looks like this because nearly three–quarters of the Earth is covered by sea. If you travel the world you have to cross over many seas.

Harry and Ralph approach the coast of another country. It's lucky they remembered to bring their passports. Do you know why they need them?

They fly over northern France. They see miles of lush, rich farmland. There are apple and pear trees in the orchards and herds of dairy cows in the fields.

Can you find out about the farms in other countries in Europe?

The globe

Harry and Ralph think travelling is fun. They look at a map of the world to help them decide where to go next. It's easy to think that the world is flat like a map, but really it's round like a globe.

Harry blows up an inflatable globe.

At the top of the globe is the North Pole. The South Pole is at the bottom. An imaginary line drawn round the middle of the globe is called the equator.

equator

I can play ball with it!

The equator

Harry and Ralph look at the globe to see which places are on the equator.

They decide to visit Brazil in South America. Look at a map or a globe to find out which other countries are on the equator.

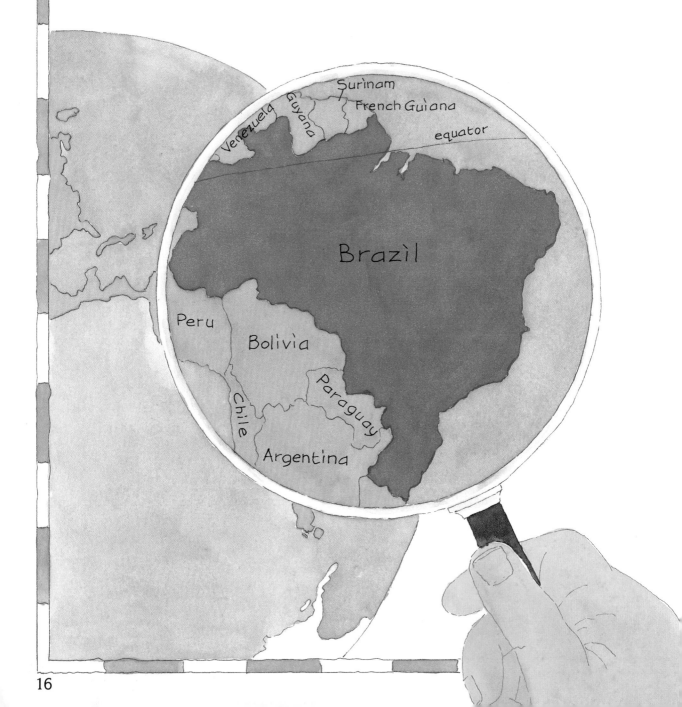

At the equator, it's hot and steamy. There are thick rainforests, with tall trees which grow close together.

The poles

Harry and Ralph are going to visit the Poles. Ralph wants to know what it's really like at the North Pole.

It's very cold because the North Pole is in the middle of the frozen Arctic Ocean. Polar bears and other animals that live at the North Pole have thick fur to keep them warm.

The South Pole is in the middle of a frozen place called Antarctica. It's the coldest place in the world.

Penguins are one of the few creatures that can survive here.

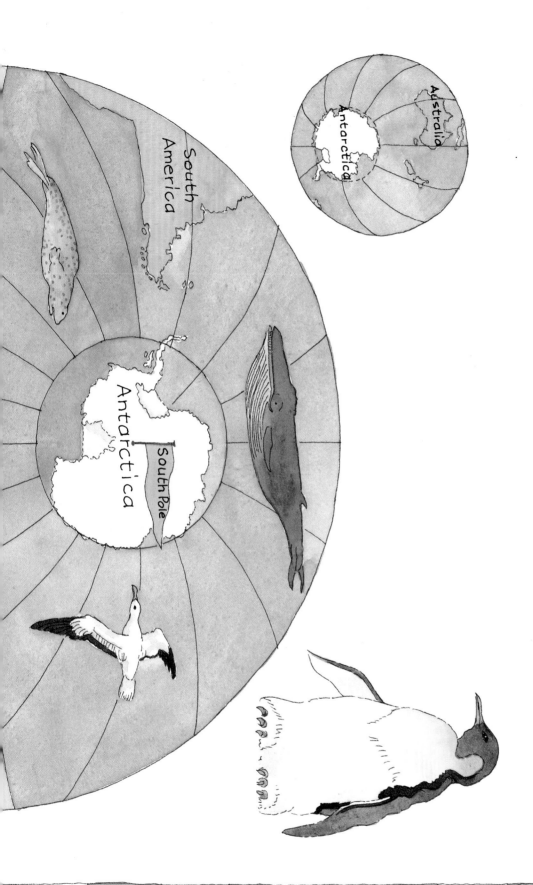

South America

Antarctica

Australia

Antarctica

South Pole

Desert and grassland

Ralph and Harry can't wait to fly to the hottest place in the world, the Sahara – a desert in Africa. They find the Sahara on the globe. The desert spreads across several African countries. Can you see which countries they are? In the Sahara, there is hot sunshine but little rain, which makes it difficult for plants to grow.

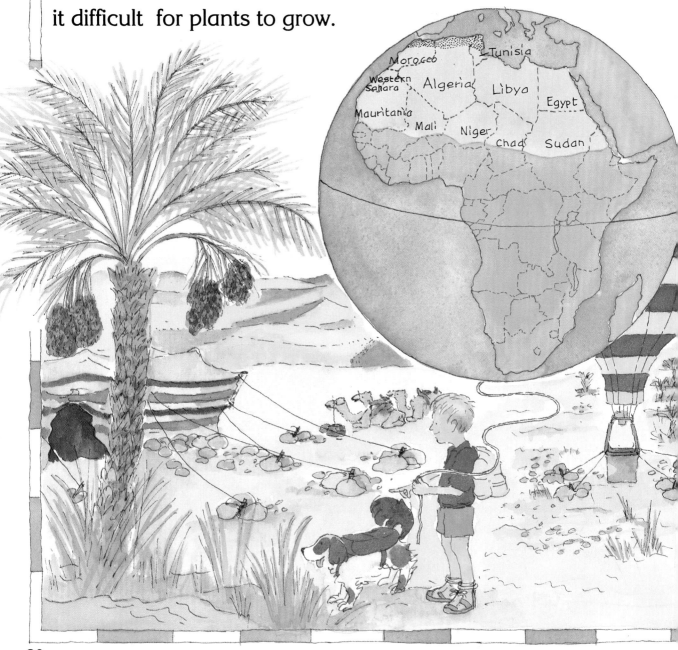

On the globe, Ralph and Harry see that below the Sahara there are flat grassy plains. They visit the wild animals roaming among the grasslands.

Don't try to round them up Ralph!

Sahara

rainforest

grasslands

The highest mountain

Harry and Ralph have visited the hottest and the coldest places in the world. They have seen the North and South Poles, the Sahara Desert, grasslands and rainforests.

Now Harry wants to visit the highest mountain, so they fly to Mount Everest which is 8,848 metres high. It is part of a group or range of mountains called the Himalayas.

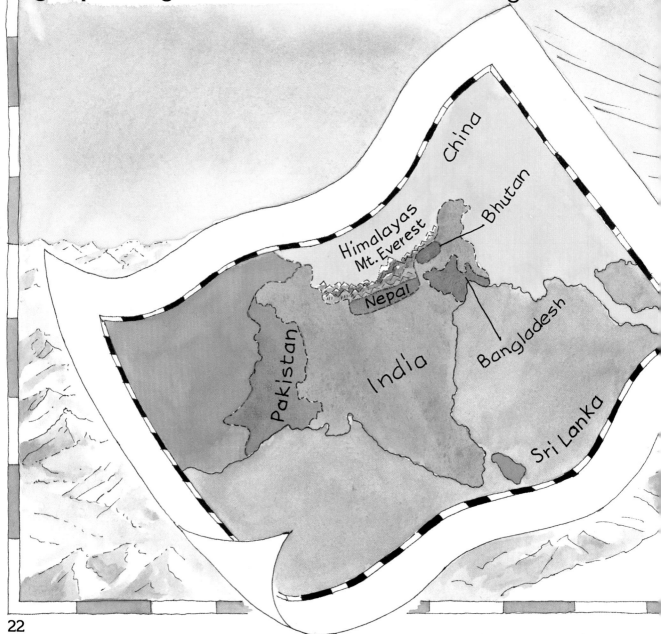

They can see the Himalaya mountains marked on the map. Mount Everest is on the border of the countries of China and Nepal.

The continents

On this map of the world, look at the six groups of countries: North America, South America, Africa, Europe, Asia and Australia. They are known as continents. Antarctica is also a continent. Which continents have Harry and Ralph visited?

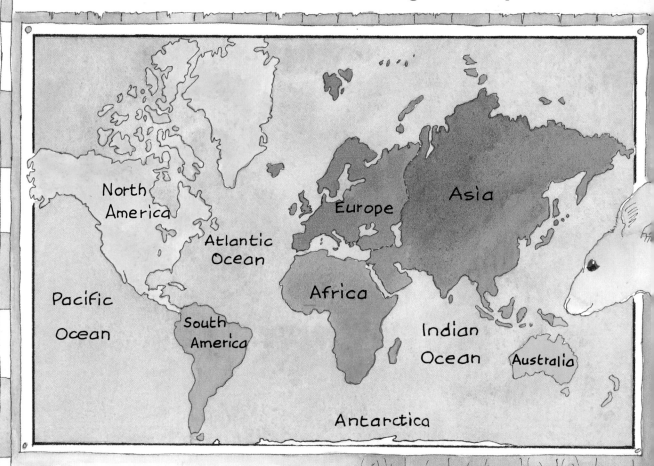

North America

Atlantic Ocean

Europe

Asia

Pacific Ocean

Africa

South America

Indian Ocean

Australia

Antarctica

Britain is a country in the continent of Europe. India is a country in the continent of Asia. But Australia is a country that is also a continent.

Can you name these Australian animals?

The countries of the world

This map shows many of the countries of the world. There are about 200 altogether so there isn't enough room to label each one.

Greenland

Norway

Sweden

Iceland

United Kingdom

Ireland

Germany

France

Italy

Spain

Alaska

Canada

U.S.A.

West Indies

Mexico

There ar
52 count
in

Brazil

Peru

Bolivia

Paraguay

Chile

Uruguay

Argentina

Falkland Islands

Picture Atlas of the World

World Atlas

Try to find the biggest country in the world. Then try to find the country where you live. Compare them for size.

Harry looks at maps and books to help him find out more about the different countries of the world.

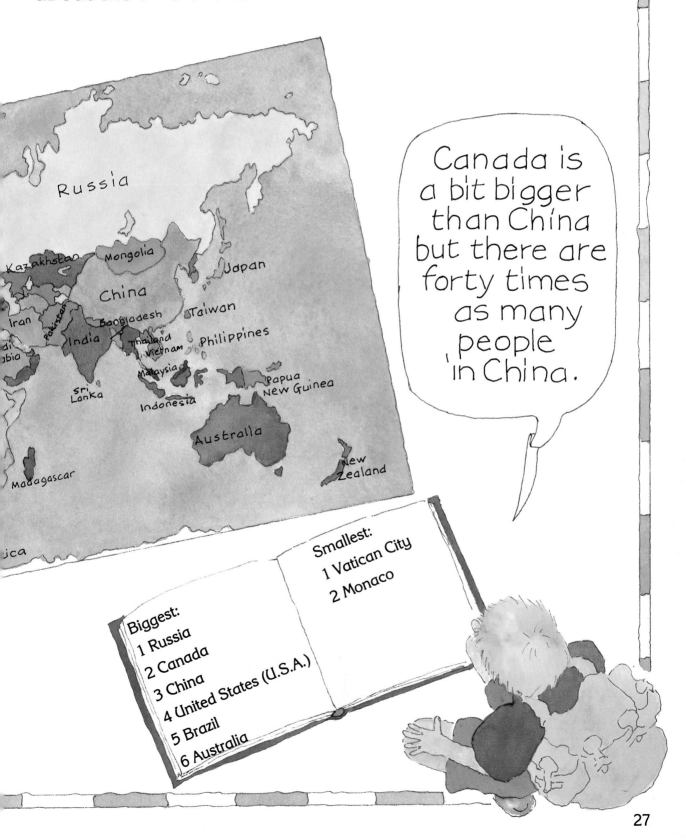

Russia

Kazakhstan   Mongolia

China   Japan

Iran   Taiwan

Bangladesh   Philippines

India   Thailand
Vietnam
Malaysia
Pakistan

Sri
Lanka   Papua
New Guinea

Indonesia

Madagascar

Australia

New
Zealand

Canada is a bit bigger than China but there are forty times as many people in China.

Smallest:
1 Vatican City
2 Monaco

Biggest:
1 Russia
2 Canada
3 China
4 United States (U.S.A.)
5 Brazil
6 Australia

27

People of the world

Maps and globes can tell you a lot about the countries of the world but they can't tell you much about the people who live there.

Harry and Ralph are trying to find out how people from other countries live and what languages they speak. They have made a questionnaire. Harry has filled in one about Ralph. Now he's filling in one for himself.

Language: English
Home: brick house
Transport: bike, hot air balloon
Favourite food: chips pizza

Language: barking
Home: kennel
Transport: hot air balloon
Favourite food: bones

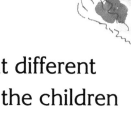

You can look at books and pictures about different countries and fill in questionnaires about the children who live there.

Index

This index will help you to find some of the important words in the book.